One other witness, Mr. Offer, complained chiefly of exactions in the shape of fees to the City, representing that many Ship-brokers were not licensed, that it was unnecessary in the character of "Ship Agents," but having given in his bond security for payment of the annual rent, he necessarily continued an admitted Broker. This evidence may be dismissed with the reply;—that on proper representations being made by persons ceasing to act as Brokers, no obstacles are raised by the City Court to the cancelling of the Bonds and the erasure of their names from the list of Brokers.

The evidence of the Stockbroker requires more special attention. The figures given have reference to the Report of the Royal Commission, and to the Index analysis of the Blue book which will show that the statements of the witness were of so diffuse a character that it is scarcely possible to follow them closely in any criticism. They may be classed under two heads, or statements affecting the Court of Aldermen, and statements with respect to the Stock Exchange. These two subjects are mixed up in an almost apparently intentional rambling manner of giving evidence, and lead to many false inferences, if the witness is not absolutely open to the charge of misrepresentation. Mr. Jos. Laurence, sworn on the 9th December, 1853, and representing himself as deputed by a body of 800 associated members of the Stock Exchange, objected to the City privilege on the grounds of having fallen into abeyance (4060). That no appeals are made to the City Court (4072). That it serves no other purpose than raising a revenue, a useless exaction (4077). That it was only created to provide compensation for abolished offices (4078). The witness twice stated that he never heard of a case investigated by the City, except to compel payment of rents and penalties (4060), except in the case of some public default (4072). The exact latitude taken by the witness in his definition of "public default" in qualifying his positive statements need not be enquired into. But the fact is, that the Press reported the two cases of L. le Grande and — Lodge, both members of the Stock Exchange, under investigation of the Court of Aldermen on the 10th December, the day after Mr. Laurence appeared before the Commission. Many earlier cases can be given, as that of Rochas and Son, and more recently, Wm. Toovey Gooch, and Edward Newton Bryant, deceased. Moreover in the copy of the Form of Summons to the Court of Aldermen, given by Mr. Serjt. Mereweather (4985), the roll of business contains several petitions against Stockbrokers, dated from 15 to 6 days previous to the evidence of the witness, and one of these was presented by Sir R. W. Carden, himself a member of the Stock Exchange, against a Stockbroker who has since become a member of the Stock Exchange.

As a further and sufficient reply, Mr. Serjeant Mereweather

testifies to—"about 20 or 30 cases since he held office (5201) one "or two a year lately more numerous," and he particularly alludes to speculation on the Stock Market as the cause of complaints increasing (5202). He adds, the jurisdiction is beneficial (5203) and Lord Campbell's approval of the system (5214).

Mr. Laurence objected to the payments exacted by the City (4080 4083) stating his own payments many years back, and is *unwillingly* forced to admit his knowledge that these payments for the freedom had been recently modified. But even this matter could not affect the principle involved in the beneficial jurisdiction contemplated by the Acts of William III and 6th Anne.

The witness asserts that the City Regulations on the subject of Stockbrokers date from the 6th Anne (4076), "*Strictly* the object "of the Legislsture was *not* to give any protection to the public in "respect to dealings on the Stock Exchange" (4078) He doubts the legality of the City claim to jurisdiction over Stockbrokers—those *now* exercising the office of Stockbrokers do not come within the meaning of the term as clearly defined in the Statute of 6th Anne, "dealing in Government Annuities," "*a snecies of property* "*not even in existence at the time of the Act of Anne,* 1707."* Though naïvely admitting the case had been decided against them by the Court of Queen's Bench (4087 & 4073), yet, if Stockbrokers called themselves "Agents" or "Factors," the City would have no pretext (4085), and the words of the witness in the body of the Report are, "There is another very strong point "on this subject in confirmation of the view that the terms of the "Act must be strictly adhered to; that in the *subsequent* Act, 8 "& 9, Wm. III., when enactments were made which intended to "include *other* persons than Brokers *so designated,* additional "words were introduced into the Act, and they were described as "Brokers and Stock Jobbers" (4077), alleging that this confirms the view that if the Legislature had intended to enlarge the description of parties they would have used terms wide enough to designate them. The witness thus admitting his knowledge of this special and experimental Act, ought, in honesty, to have given the entire words in the preamble of the Act, which are, "Brokers, Stock Jobbers, and *pretended Brokers,*" or the enlarged description of parties thus stigmatized and repudiated, that they have unlawfully "combined and confederated," and defines Brokers as being concerned in any "Government Talleys," &c., "Bills or Stock of the Bank of England, or for or concerning "any part or share of the Capital or Joint Stock belonging to or

* A Parliamentary paper printed in 1859, shews that the 1st funded loan was contracted with the Bank of England in in 1694—that a *second loan was contracted in the 5 & 6 Anne,* raising the debt to £5,064,263 in the earlier part of this year—and that the funded debt of the country was £43,371,864 in 1717. The first issue of South Sea Stock, to the amount of £9,177,968, was in 1712.

"to belong to any Company or Society that is, or shall be incor-"porated by Act of Parliament or Letters Patent." The simple word "Brokers" only being used throughout the clauses of the Act. By an Act of the same year—8 & 9 Wm. III. c. 20. § 60—they are also designated Brokers, thus "Brokers" for the buying and selling of Tallies, &c., taking more than 2s. 6d. per cent commission, &c. And by the 10th Anne, c. 19, § 121, (known as the Cards and Dice Act), which is ***subsequent,*** and enacts a penalty of £20 against any "Broker or Brokers" who may take or receive, directly or indirectly, more than 2s. 9d per cent. for buying or selling "any share or interest in any *Joint Stock* created by Act "of Parliament or by Letters Patent."

These enactments, showing how stringently and specially Stock Brokers had been made the subject of legislation, remaining amongst the penal Statutes which the Stock Exchange have associated themselves to evade, were not brought under the notice of the Commission. The Stock Exchange contends that the last of these Acts can be retrospective only at a date when no other than Government Securities were known, that Share Agents and Factors are not Stock Brokers nor yet Brokers. Conveniently ignoring the existence of Mercantile Trading Companies, carried on by the Dutch, Portuguese, Danes, Brandenburgers, and the French; the failure projects in Scotland! and the existence in England of the rival East India Companies, &c., including the African Trading Company, with Acts and Charters under 16th James I., Charles I., Charles II., 1662 & 1672, trading till 1697, when the monoply was thrown open for thirteen years, save in the 10 per cent. duties granted to the Company, within which period—1697 and 1710, the exact dates of the first and last of the Acts regulating Stock Brokers—the Directors were charged with raising £180,000 additional capital, and dividing that sum, and more, besides profits, amongst the shareholders. They ignore, also, the mania of the period, and the swindles of projectors, finally terminated for a century by Parliament in 1720. These are described graphically with "Flying Ship" and Insurance of Nose" Companies, &c. and the concomitant parties of Brokers and Stock Jobbers, with practices followed to this day, in the pamphlet "Exchange Alley; "or, The Stock Jobber turn'd Gentleman:" "Humbly inscribed "to the Gentlemen daily attending Jonathan's Coffee House."

The witness might also be further met by the proof against his assertion that Stock Brokers are not Brokers in the exemption of Cattle, Corn, Coal, and Provision *Salesmen,* from being esteemed Brokers under the Act William III.

The witness is forced to admit that the City Regulations do not "*clash*" with the rules of the Stock Exchange, except in the one case of the passing the names of principals (4071). This is impossible to be done *in dealings of the Stock Exchange;* they deal with a class of persons called *Jobbers*, who are not principals, and to whom the names of the principals are never given (4058 & 4059). The motives for this statement were not elicited by the Commission, and will therefore be shewn in dealing with the rules and practices of the Stock Exchange, when it may also be seen that the members of this Society have confederated to take advantage of all penal disabilities against non-members, to evade legal engagements, and to obstruct the fulfilment of this stringent requirement of the law,

The ridicule which the witness attempted to raise with respect to the Cabman's Badge, &c., (4087), might be characterised as only frivolous, had these statements not been introduced for the purpose of misleading and diverting the attention of the Commission. He admits that the City has varied the Regulations (4076), that it is never exercised (4088), and the complaints of the witness have at length been reduced to his feeling it a degradation to sign an engagement which is, that they will keep certain books they prescribe (4058), and "now" only to perform justly the duties of their office (4089), or, if these Regulations are a "little differing" from the rules the City prescribe to Brokers in goods, &c. (4058), it is believed to be only in following more closely the Act of William III. and adopting the words of the oath, which are without "*fraud and collusion*," which many of them, says the witness, feel a "great hardship"—consciences grievously offended by clauses of the bond which they find themselves unable to fulfil (4088) explaining that "persons, of course, "have less objection to sign a bond that they will pay the "penalty;" a strange admission of the truth, that, except for a salutary fear of exposure and disqualification by the City, the payment of the penalty would be risked as a speculation, under the countenance of the Committee administering the rules of the Society by whom "the City Regulations are set aside" (4066) by the superadded regulations of the Stock Exchange (4072).

"Thus—those are wealthy who but dare to cheat."

The anachronism in the reigns of sovereigns was, perhaps, thought worthless as an argument against the witness: but, on reading this weak evidence, it may be asked—If, on Reporting so strongly, the Commission has not been guided by pre-conceived prejudices of leaving all matters of trade unhampered, even in the special case of a class notoriously organized to resist all legal authority; or, that the Commission has been deceived by such a statement as—that these observations apply more or less to all Brokers, but the case of Stock Brokers is *stronger!* (4086); or, such irrelevant statements as—persons not producing the obsolete Cabman's Badge "are really liable to the penalty of £1,000." (4089); whereas it was in William III. the common penalty of

40s.: that the calculation of the amount of fees for 150 years is now enormous! and that "the 6th Anne was to stop informers", (4075) "under the Act James I, which was found not only useless but mischievous" (4077), that is, the garbling of spices!

The acuteness of the Commission must have suspected that the mind of the witness, in appealing to the feeling of contempt for informers, was dwelling upon the knowledge of many good and stronger grounds of information against members of the Association known as the Stock Exchange. And the Commission must have perceived that the words, "freedom of trade," the "spirit "of freedom," applied to these mild and simple Regulations of the City, as being inconsistent with the "position" of the parties on whom they are imposed, were an abuse of popular phrases, and meant freedom of licence to confederate to trade in a way which had been denounced.

Before bringing forward the second head of the witness' evidence, having reference to the Stock Exchange, one statement requires to be noticed. In saying that a Broker expelled by the Committee could no longer be a member of the Stock Exchange with a "*certificate of respectability*," but might freely exercise his office elsewhere (4069), he is asked if "he acts in the Rotunda?" and replies, "he acts outside" (4070). It must be explained that the Rotunda was a chamber formerly kept open in the Bank of England for the resort of fundholders, to transact business through the City Licensed Brokers. A clause had been inserted in the Bank Act of 1834 to shut this chamber; without, perhaps, the Government being aware that thereby was closed the only semblance of an *open* market for the exchange and transfer of Government Stocks. The Commission, by the question, seemed to be unaware of the fact; and Mr. Lawrence, to say the least, evades the question most disingenuously.

It remains to be added that Mr. Lawrence was written to and informed that an attempt would be made to contradict his evidence, and the inferences which might be drawn from his statements having reference to the Stock Exchange; yet the witness made no subsequent appearance to correct his evidence. He had already gained one step in an impudent attempt towards getting the Stock Exchange recognised as a public body: a position which they were not slow to take advantage of, in asserting a locus standi before parliament. On Feb. 19th, 1858, a petition from the association was presented by Sir George Grey to the House of Commons, praying for the abolition of the city jurisdiction over Brokers, and supported by Mr. T. Baring, who was subsequently invited by them to stand for the representation of the City. They trusted, no doubt, to the select Committee, on the Bill being debarrred from hearing further evidence, as it can scarcely be presumed that any member of the Association would have presented himself to maintain the evidence of Mr. Lawrence, or to be cross-examined upon the organisation and the rules of the Stock Exchange.

It may not be also too much to allege that the Commission, in refusing to hear another witness, and abstaining from a well directed inquiry from this witness, assisted the interests of the Association he represented, in the suppression of as much as possible, regarding its constitution, and the motives for confederation, whilst the Commission may, perhaps, be thought to show a bias in the reception of evidence without contradiction from the mode of putting a question to a witness on the next sitting. Mr. A. Moore is asked, "Do you think it necessary that there should be any "authority to control Stockbrokers, for example: *Except the "Committee of the Stock Exchange, what object does it answer, "except to produce a revenue?* the witness replies, there is an im-"portant safe-guard in the City control (4331) and in cases of frau-"dulent Brokers, there is every disposition to prosecute, but has "observed that these men generally abscond."

The remaining charges against the City are brought forward by the witness in direct opposition to his representations of the Stock Exchange; that fraudulent bankrupts are admitted by the City, (4064 & 4065) and that the City bond would be forfeited to the City use (4090 & 4092) But Mr. Serjeant Merryweather expressly says, "an applicant is asked if he has been a bankrupt, or unsuc-"cessful in trade, and enquiries are made." (5214) And Alderman Wire testifies to a case in which the Corporation divided a fine of £10,000 amongst sufferers from the delinquencies of the man who paid the fine. (7959) Of the Stock Exchange, Mr. Lawrence says that a searching inquiry is made into character; a member is obliged to find three securities, not only for pecuniary payment, in case of default (4054) qualified perhaps in a subsequent reply, "sufficient security *to the body of which he is a member*," which goes to the payment of any loss that may be incurred by his creditors. (4063) The unstated fact is, that these securities are required only for *two years*, and the pecuniary payment in default is *exclusively* for the benefit of the body of which he is a member. Of a similar nature is the statement that in those cases of public default brought before the City anything like redress from the friends of the party had already been *exhausted* by the Stock Exchange (4072) When it is added that all redress in these cases is EXCLUSIVELY exhausted by the Stock Exchange, the words may not be received in the sense in which it is presumed they were accepted by the Commission, after being told that the present system (of the City) affords no security to the public with respect to transactions on the Stock Exchange, beyond that which is already provided by the Committee and the *Common Law*. (4063) And that the Committee act not only as a Court of *Law*, or even of Equity, but as a Court of Honour. (4068.) The Commission are drawn deeper into an unsound deduction by replies to their own final questions; "That if a sum of money is deposited in the "hands of a Broker, were appropriated to his own use, the City "Bond would be forfeited?" (4090) "*And the bond to the Stock "Exchange?*" when the actual words of the witness are "QUITE "so." (4091)

The Committee of this association exclude general creditors, not only from participation in the benefits of the bond, whilst it exists, but also from the division of the assets collected in the Association from the debtors of the defaulter, throwing upon them all the disabilities of the Statutory Law. They seize at the same time all the property or money of these creditors within their reach. And the Association is only too successful under this impudent assumption of authority in even a FRAUDULENT APPROPRIATION, where there is no disability in the public sufferer, except ignorance of his rights, or his unwillingness to risk a law suit against a strong confederation, ready to assist members in defending actions to the extent of instructing solicitors under their own legal advisers, resisting to the moment of going into court, yielding only to avoid exposure and collision, or carrying it into court where, from technicalities or disabilities, they may gain a judgment recorded to their future advantage.

The Association may attempt to deny this exclusion of the claims of outside creditors; the fact is, that at one time a positive law of the Association, forbade any participation, but a Lombard Street Banker, on one occasion threatening to take out a fiat in bankruptcy against the defaulter, his claim was admitted, years afterwards, and when this circumstance had become known, the former rule was expunged, and a new rule inserted in their printed code, which is even now only *permissive.* Thus:—

(Rule 160) "Parties not members of the Stock Exchange, "MAY, *with the consent of the Creditors, be allowed* an equal "participation of assets; subjects to the same conditions as mem-"bers, and any one whose claim is admitted, shall have the right "to be represented at the meeting of creditors by any member of "the House he may select."

Participation is generally resisted, and only unwillingly conceded to powerful or restive parties, who may threaten legal proceedings. The practice may be shown by two cases which occurred in November and December 1857—In the case of the default of J. B · · · · · · who held a deposit from a client as security against loss on a speculative account; participation was with difficulty obtained in the dividend derived from this deposit, the only asset. In the case of J. D · · · · · the client had sold £1200 worth of Great Western Stock, and bought Stock of the same value of the Great Northern Railway. He delivered the Stock sold to his broker, who *declared himself* a defaulter the same afternoon. The proceeds of the sale (included in the defaulter's account, and also the sole amount and asset) was paid over to the Stock Exchange, assignees, who called upon this client to pay a *difference* loss upon the uncompleted purchase, in this case also participation was in the first instance refused; it was at length granted on the creditor signing an agreement to accept the Stock Exchange composition and to waive all further legal claims.

These cases would probably not have occurred but for the rule (155) of the Association, requiring every member of the Stock Exchange to "pay at least one-third of the balance of any loss" to be eligible for re-admission. *A direct inducement to a fraudulent preference* of the Association, and this may probably be found to occur in a majority of cases where the defaulter acting as a Broker has "outside" clients and creditors.

Both these cases might have had redress for recovery in full —one under Sir J. Barnard's Act, the other by a fiat in Bankruptcy (or proceeding upon fraud) at his single instance, and involving, no doubt, an action at law against the Stock Exchange assignees, already unsuccessfully attempted in the matter of Nicholson *v.* Gooch, or the assignees of bankruptcy against the assignee of the Stock Exchange.

It is, moreover, known that had this decision been adverse to the Association, it was intended that their assignee should resort to the Insolvent Court to obtain release and was to be immediately re-admitted, notwithstanding their rules rendering persons taking the benefit of the Insolvent Act ineligible for membership.

The Stock Exchange under their regulations treat all incomplete transactions, whether bonâ fide purchases or sales, as gambling. On the default of a member all open accounts are closed. The differences against the outside clients are often struck at extremely unfavourable prices, from the defaulting Broker having given previous information to his inside creditors of his intended default, by a preference increasing to the utmost the claims of the members, to secure his re-election, in permitting them to make up their accounts favourably, and "to make a market" for his outside clients, both at this compulsory closing of the accounts. And also in an extreme price, should they require to re-open them; giving the members a large jobbing profit between the original price and that of the second contract. Any claim upon the second contract is totally ignored by the Committee of the Association, and should there be any such claim against the principal, or the Broker in the character of principal, presuming it capable of being made good in law, with all the disabilities of the rules and practice of the Association, by refusing the principal, they leave it against the Broker, whom they have denuded of his banker's balance and all his effects within their reach.

A case to which there is no parallel in ordinary trade. The

compulsory closing of a purchase within closed doors, without notice and without power given of protection to the client of his property. A clique of Jobbers making a "rigged" market both for the sale and the re-purchase with total repudiation of any loss on the second purchase, held by the Committee as having no reference to the first contract, which was treated and closed as a gambling transaction.

The Society has a rule requiring defaulting members to surrender their books, and of course, *the names of their principals*; and the Committee is generally successful in collecting these losses, however much exaggerated, from debtors who are able to pay, under threats of exposure and posting in their "Black Book." By these means, the appropriation of deposit monies and trust funds and setting at defiance the claims of creditors outside, the Society, as a body collectively, gain largely on balance against losses sustained by the repudiation of outside speculators, even under the operation of Sir J. Barnard's Act, which is applicable only to Government Stocks. Recurring now to the only point in which the City rules "*clash*"—the difficulty of the witness of the Commission in passing the names of principals to Jobbers to whom "*the* names are never given" (4058 & 4059) Its origin may be seen in the procedure of the Committee to gain assets for division, and in the profits obtained by the Jobbers in buying and re-selling. That whilst the Jobbers do not accept the names of principals during the solvency of the Broker, they have the full benefit of them on the surrender of the books and enjoy the benefit of repudiation under the countenance of the Committee. The witness says, "a Broker employed by one merchant to purchase goods, "may buy them at *public auction* without the intervention of "another Broker. On the Stock Exchange *the duty is only to* "*one party, he owes no duty to the other*" (4084). To which party does the witness mean? might be sarcastically asked. Biassed by his personal interests and sympathies, he obviously discloses the duty he wishes to owe to his confederates, protection from all legal liability to fulfil their contracts, protection for a second jobbing profit, protection for character under the administration of the Committee; this duty he owes imperatively to the Committee, and is the only difficulty of the position in which he is placed by the superadded rules of the Society.

The Stock Exchange is a closed market, pregnant with facilities for collusion, having no pretence to comparison with an Auction Mart. The importance of the subject, especially on the Stock Exchange, is clearly shewn in the Report of a trial, Kensington Lewis *v.* Lloyd (Feb. 1838). Mr. John Capel replies that "a "Broker is bound by his oath to give you the person he buys and "sells stock to." Mr. Serjeant Wilde (Lord Truro) asks, "if "this is not done, is it in the power of the Broker to bring for-

"ward a beggar if it is a gaining concern, and a rich man if it is "losing concern?" an allegation which was made by the plaintiff's counsel in the circumstances which led to this trial.

The practice of the Association is to be found in the Report of the Committee of the House of Commons on the Exchequer Bills Forgery Inquiry.

Mr. Hutchinson says, "we never name the principal on the "Stock Exchange, *we give to the principals out of the house the* "*names of the dealers in the house*" (4187). Mr. Pearce, the chairman, says, "It is very well known generally, in dealing with "parties who are the Brokers of respectable bankers AND SO ON, "that in dealing with those Brokers they are dealing with those "bankers." Mr. Hutchinson (V.C.) begs further to elucidate this, by instancing the example of a party refusing to go on with a loan on the forged Exchequer Bills; and adds "if a person is "agent for a banker it is well known." Mr. C. Keyser says, "Yes, if any persons had been asked for whom Morgans were "borrowing money, they would have answered, 'for Ransoms.'" (3031 & 3032).

Such is the actual evidence given—amongst others, by Mr. Laurence's own partner—when the representation in this light suited the purpose of the Association. It is a full answer to the statement to the Commission, that the passing of names is "*highly* "*improper.*" And the instancing of the Bank of England, certainly, if not the most impudent, was the least tenable of all the positions of the witness; that corporation only doing legitimate business, which is bruited about and known to all the Stock Exchange, and when acting on Government account the amount is immediately reported by the press; yet the witness professes not to speak of "irregular practices on the Stock Exchange, or of "anything approaching to gambling, but *the regular mode of* "*dealing.*" (4059).

The Stock Exchange have also availed themselves of the names of principals: in the case of Grisewood *v.* Blane, the plaintiff sued the client of a defaulting Broker. And so recently as February, 1860, in the case of Soilleux *v.* Innocent, the plaintiff himself a defaulter, probably suing for the benefit of the assignees of the Stock Exchange, and who had two days previously obtained a verdict against a client of his own, swore that as a Jobber he had *always known* the name of the principal, whilst the defendant had no knowledge of him and had in part paid the intermediate Broker. The witness was also well aware of the fact that the Brokers of the Stock Exchange do avail themselves of the benefits of giving the names of the Jobbers to their clients, and throw upon them the losses from the defaults of these principals; although some of the most reputable forego this, or when a stipulation has been required of them by previous arrangements, probably feeling that they are bound by the rules of the Society to give their clients no option of rejecting these principals, and that they are also bound by their rules to obstruct their clients from holding any of their associates to their engagements.

But a case can be given where a Broker paid his client the amount of a composition, and yet was known to have a "set-offe in his accounts with the defaulter, of which he did not give his client the benefit, thereby making a profit by the default.

In the recent panic of May, 1859, and disgraceful failure of more than seventy members of the Stock Exchange, this was done in cases where the names had not been given on the contract or declared previous to the default; and one Broker went so far, and so general was the default of his Jobbers, as to have his books made up by a Public Accountant; he deducted the Accountant's as well as the Stock Exchange Assignee's charge from these compositions, but afforded his clients no means of knowing his profits in "sets-off," nor would they have access to information or be recognised by the Committee to obtain participation in any future dividends. In one case, where he paid the client a *smaller composition* than was understood to have been received from the defaulter, *the Committee refused to entertain any complaint.*

In this general default of 1859, as it may be called, from the Committee granting time to all members who might pay 10s. in the pound, and declaring no defaults after the first 3 or 4 days, it is well known that members had themselves declared to close their accounts and evade their contracts; many of these, who made no payments beyond their banker's balance and the differences collected in the Association, were instantly re-admitted and protected by the Committee. If re-admission was delayed, it was probably in cases of Brokers to force them to sue for claims against outside defaulters for the benefit of the Association, or in other cases where the Brokers were deterred from presenting themselves under fear of legal proceedings from their clients for breaches of trust or irregularities.

A member of the body recently lodged a claim against the estate of another member in the Court of Bankruptcy, and was opposed on the grounds of the Association having assets from which they excluded the Court creditors. The claimant was admitted conditionally to not receiving more than the bankruptcy creditors. It would seem, therefore, that the Stock Exchange have gained the option of holding their own assets or the taking a larger benefit under this Court.

After the panic of 1859, a member applied in the Court of Bankruptcy to take out a fiat against another, stating that he had the sanction of the Committee. The loss had arisen from the depreciation of property held as security for a loan. At the same time the Committee expelled an old member, retired from active business, who had protected himself under similar circumstances, by arresting his debtors funds at his bankers, which the Committee required for division amongst the difference claimants on his after default. Had the holder of the pawned securities sold them for his own use, or delivered them over to the Committee for general division on his own default, the Committee would have treated the matter only as a difference account, and would have controlled their defrauded member from taking legal proceedings.

From the evidence given by members before the Exchequer Bill Forgery Committee, may be shewn the regulations of the Society with respect to going to law with each other. Mr. Hutchinson is asked, "Is it against the rules of the Stock Exchange "that parties should go to law, or must such matters be settled by "the Committee?" and replies, "If by going to law the object "was to gain a preference over any other creditor, if he did by "that process obtain more than others, the Committee would "insist upon its being divided; and if he refused, the Committee "would expel him" (4186).

This rank evasion of a plain question, and ingenious casuistry of giving an equitable and legal turn to the most strict regulation of the Association, is best met by another and more straightforward member. Mr. J. L. Wolfe says, "*We cannot* proceed "against each other at law while on the Stock Exchange. The Committee takes the matter off our hands" (306, 308). The Committee have had difficulty in controlling their own members at times. On one occasion, a member preferred a charge of fraud against another at the Mansion House; after two or three adjournments the affair was quashed, under compulsion of the Committee. The daily Press gave no report of the proceedings.

Mr. C. J. Brown states that the Stock Exchange Committee followed up the forged Exchequer Bills to the last member—"we "cannot follow further" (718). The inability to follow further is inherent to a strictly private association, and the investigation of all matters affecting the conduct and character of members under a secret tribunal, is also an inherent motive for the confederation of the body. This shews, also, the purely protective nature of their regulations. The Committee do not wish to follow such matters farther—they leave the last member to seek redress at the Common Law: they do not even investigate his conduct; and should he have originated the forgery or fraud, he would escape by making pecuniary restitution to other members; or, should unavoidable publicity require a scapegoat, an *inferior* member would be expelled; whilst equally guilty, but more *influential* members would escape. This has been asserted even in the notorious Exchequer Bills forgery case, and that the conduct of four members was not investigated, their names not having been prominently brought forward in the official and public investigation.

Further proofs of the policy of the Association to compromise felony and to exercise the unlimited power of the Committee over members, to avoid exposure and sustain the character of the Association, will be seen in cases given presently to shew the administration of the governing Committee. The most practical and satisfactory way of meeting the general statements of the witness, and the strong pressure laid by him upon the "certificate "of respectability conferred by membership" (4069); "there "are securities, recommending in point of character" (4054); "there is a searching enquiry, three securities, *members*, them-"selves known, attend to answer inquiries" (4066, 4067). "The "Committee have *unlimited* power; they act not only as a Court "of *Law, or even of Equity, but as a court of honor!* They have "the power of expulsion for misconduct" (4068).

The rules of the Association are only stringent against the public. It is well understood that *they have a reservation in favor of the members*, unless in the arbitrary dictation to submit to the decisions of the Committee to avoid collision with the Courts of Law. Three regulations only—with respect to the admission of members—in addition to those already noticed, may be given, and the code need not again be referred to. The Committee require every candidate for admission to sign a declaration that he is not in business, (or his wife). The motive for this abortive rule is to avoid collision with the Court of Bankruptcy. Another rule renders parties who have been bankrupts ineligible for two years after obtaining a certificate: members have, however, been admitted within the required period of probation. There is also a rule rendering persons who have taken the benefit of the Insolvent Act incapable of being elected: a Broker with a large speculative business tempted a very poor member of the Society, by a bribe of £20, to accept a transfer, and register a large number of shares in the Vale of Neath Railway Company; he went through the Insolvent Court to evade the calls subsequently falling due, and was re-admitted; this Broker occupying the chair on the day of his re-election.

The admission of members is not regulated on principle of character, but entirely of exclusiveness. But this being well-understood, it is of more importance to shew the character of the qualifications of persons who have been admitted.

The witness was well-aware that stringent inquiries are made with reference more to the jealousies and enmities of existing members, and to the influence of the candidates' connexions. It is often said that one of the most certain means of obtaining admission is a threat of exposure of irregularities over members who, under coercion, consent to propose and to canvass for the applicant. Certain Brokers are supposed to introduce parties to serve the purpose of lending their names at any time, for a small fee, as principals, when called for in transactions accurately described in 1720 in the "Stock Broker turn'd Gentlemen":

"*Lady Speculator*—Mr. Cheat, buy for me at 100 against to-"morrow."

"*Cheat (aside)*—The price is 90; I'll pocket the 10 per cent. "If it rises beyond the price limited, I'll then transfer it as my "own, and pretend I've been disappointed in buying. If it falls, "the loss is hers."

A collusive process much facilitated by the close market of the Stock Exchange.

A leading member of the Committee, it is believed, was on one occasion about to propose a defaulter in a country market, a client of his own, and to forgive a debt of £4,000, the more conscientiously to speak of his credit and character; he desisted, probably, from the circumstances being too well-kn wn in the locality by parties whose election he had unscrupulously opposed, from jealousy and personal animosity. Persons deeply in debt to members have been brought into the Association by the influence of creditors, from the hope of being ultimately paid. A case can be given of the election of a party who had changed the spelling of his name, and had many protested bills and debts in another market in London.

In the Court of Bankruptcy, Mr. Mark Boyd stated, that on the name of his clerk being posted for election, he sent a protest to the Committee: the name *was taken down*, and yet the party was elected. The Commissioner of the Court remarked, "*What! "do you say your clerk was elected, when he had robbed you of "more than £2,000?*"

That this party had sinister influence over members of the Committee for past transactions, or could bring a connection whose business was worth "*jobbing*" upon, are the alternative inferences to be drawn from his clandestine admission.

The two brothers G · · · · · · · · were expelled for *fraudulent and disgraceful practices:* in six months they were re-admitted, and shortly afterwards were defaulters in the panic of 1857. The Committee cannot always carry out their power of expulsion: on one occasion, a member, known to one of the metropolitan constituencies, being a shareholder in the Joint Stock capital of the buildings, threatened to force his way in by the aid of the police —they were obliged to rescind their vote. Two members of high standing and supposed wealth have recently been *allowed to retire* from the Association. It is believed that one of these escaped prosecution, from the powerful influence of a certain religious persuasion presiding in a Joint Stock Company, and from Stock Exchange sympathies.

Instances may be given of the mode in which the Committee censure their members. Some years ago, Messrs. Barclay's sent them a remonstrance—their clerk had absconded, leaving a deficiency of £5,000, abstracted at various periods. A censure was voted on the member who had given so large facilities to any one in the position of a clerk. A recommendatory resolution was also passed, and forwarded to the banker and to *The Times*. Two days afterwards, a Board Meeting, hastily summoned—when the censured member's friends were mustered—rescinded the vote. A party in town accounted for his absence from the second meeting by saying, he had voted once, and saw no occasion to record his vote again.

Some years ago, the chairman was required to cancel certain bargains, and was, moreover, suspended for a fortnight. At the expiration of that time, and the next ordinary meeting, that individual took the chair.

Of the coercion exercised by the secret inquisition of the Committee, something may be perceived occasionally in public cases. In November, 1851, the clerk of Mr. J. C——— was committed for defrauding his employer. Mr. C———, at first stated that other parties in the Stock Exchange were implicated: this he retracted on the final examination. *The Times* did not publish the first statement, but gave a lengthened report of the retractation, with Sir R. W. Carden's remarks On one occasion, this alderman having been too general in the severity of his remarks against "outsiders," he was obliged to explain them to the Committee, and a letter was published that these remarks had no reference to the Stock Exchange, or to the class of persons who were members; since which, the alderman has been more silent, unless in exposing the delinquencies of several outsiders, and giving opportunity to the Stock Exchange writers in *The Daily News* and *Times* City Articles, to advertise the "certificate of respectability of the Stock Exchange."

For other cases to substantiate what has been said, reference may now be made to a private journal of a party who had access to know something of the internal management of the Association, for obvious reasons the selection is made from occurrences some years ago. It states; "during the last twelve months, more swindles have occurred within the body itself than in any other mercantile community taken numerically in any part of the world, or during any period of mercantile pressure or distress. And this without taking into account those delinquencies so frequently brought about by Stock Exchange dealings, from which, if not actually promoted by members, as in the ——— case, they yet knowingly reap the plunder. These cases are almost invariably quashed, and public justice is defeated. Recently, the clerk of Mr. K · · · · · escaped, being the nephew of a Committee-man, Mr. F · · · · · , and also a connexion of the R · · · · · · · 's. Mr. K . . . . . after going some length, declined to prosecute;

"many parties urged proceedings, seeing the necessity of making a "single scape-goat. Mr. K · · · · · · 's silencing answer to one "of these was; Were you prosecuted in the £1500 Exchequer "bill affair?"

"Mr. S · · · · · · 's clerk has also escaped. And in the case "of a check forgery on ——— & Co, which these bankers have "told the member they shall continue to debit to his account, "(£962 10s.) the member is at large more than suspected. "Another case within these few days has been brought before the "police courts by outside sufferers; the party has since absconded"

Cases where members have been discreditably mixed up in bankruptcies need not to be mentioned, unless the reporters have been tempted to silence, they have been necessarily before the public, but the journal mentions with respect to one of these:

"That this individual was forced to admit his clerk as a partner, "to avoid the disclosure of awkward transactions."

There is, at least, one other well known party who had a partnership forced upon him under similar circumstances, and had to exert much influence to stay publicity.

With regard to breaking their most stringent laws, which hold members liable to expulsion who accept a compromise, receive payment by bills, or fail to declare every non-fulfilment of obligations, it is stated;—"In the consol settlement of this month, "(Sep. 185—) there were known to be 14 defaulters, but only "one was declared, lists of the others were *obtained by influential* "*members, and privately and confidentially shown.*"

At another date;—"On this settlement several failures were expected, but few were declared, owing, it was alleged, to some "*influential* members of the Committee being affected by the "losses. It is asserted that the bill transactions are numerous, "some of these, at long dates, have already been renewed three "times."

A short time afterwards, there is added to a list of defaults, declared and not declared, "The reason for this seeming partial- "ity, may be explained by circumstances attending the earliest of "these failures, Mr. ———. Consols were forced down about a "half per cent., from 96½ to 96 before the defaulter's account was "struck. Being a new member, the losses were required from "his securities; one of these, his uncle, resisted on the plea of the "unfair price; on remonstrance he threatened a public exposure "of the system of dealing on the Stock Exchange, and eventually, "although a very old member, retired rather than pay. Soon "after, Consols had been forced down on this occasion to 96, the "price was in the same way advanced to 96¾, when other default- "ers were declared, and their accounts closed."

A somewhat similar case of striking an account, is mentioned in the June previous to the last:—"Mr. · · · · · · · made known "his difficulties in the evening to his securities, one of whom, "Mr. · · · · · · took from him 85,000 Consols at 95⅞, after the "market had closed firmly at 96 buyers. A further rise of one-"quarter per cent. had again been established next morning "before the public announcement of the default. The outside "clients and creditors felt themselves wronged, and brought the "matter before the Committee, who, as usual, evaded the question "as one between the public and a member. *The transaction had "taken place with the sanction and concurrence of their own agent, "the Committee could investigate no further.*"

March, 185*: "Last account day, Mr. B · · · · · · was declared. "He had borrowed £1,800 from Messrs. H. & H., and £1,500 "from Mr. L., upon Bonds; which he redeemed by payment of "cheques, and sold for cash—his cheques were dishonoured. "Some of his creditors wish to make him bankrupt, but the "Committee have forbid this proceeding."

In the next month: "Mr. S · · · · · · · (formerly the keeper "of a small Eating House in Brighton) was declared. He had "bought 18 or £20,000 worth of Foreign Bonds; his cheques in "payment were dishonored; it is said his bankers were instructed "to dishonor cheques with a particular mark. His banker's "balance amounts to £7,500, his debts and differences to about "£21,000. Previous to his declaration he offered 6s. 8d. in com-"position, which his creditors refused. He now declines to "answer impertinent questions about the Bonds received; and "informs his creditors that 6s. 8d. in the pound as a composition "entitles him to return to the Stock Exchange. His creditors "have applied to his bankers, and have been told (said to be "under the advice of the defaulter's lawyer) that Mr. S. has "committed an act of bankruptcy, and therefore, the balance can "only be surrendered to assigness. Mr. S. tells his creditors that, "if they resort to bankruptcy, at the end of two years, and *per-"haps before*, he has interest to get re-elected—an elder brother "is a very wealthy member."

Within a few months of these cases, "Mr. · · · · · · failed. "He was supposed a wealthy man, and had recently bought "landed property to the amount of £15,000, which had been "settled upon his wife. He had a very large account open; but "the losses, at the prices of striking, were small, and his creditors "were afterwards paid in full. Having got into an account which "was not likely to turn out well, he adopted the course of having "himself declared, that he might get out at the smallest sacrifice."

It is worthy of note, that any member can force his own declaration; and one party, at least, is known, who made a moderate fortune by this proceeding, and continued a member.

Some of the practices of the body are shown by the Journal: "A 'rigg' has been run in Midland Stock. Parties who had "bought largely, and were heavy '*bulls,*' resorted to the ruse "of 'posting' a quantity of Stock to be bought in. It was stated "in *Herepath's Journal, that there was an understanding between "the parties that no Stock was really intended to be bought in.*" The publication of the fact caused a sensation—leading members saying, "if such was the case, that the Stock Exchange was "nothing but a monster gambling house, resorting to any practice "of the gaming table." One individual was silenced by a straightforward reply, that such was the fact, and that the member knew that similar practices were hourly and habitually practised by the body. Another alleged practice is—at the last hour a member will deal in a large amount of Railway Stock, with an understanding between the parties that the bargain is to be cancelled: an artificial closing price is thus quoted in the daily list. No cognizance of quotations in the price list is taken by the Committee, unless a complaint is lodged by a member of an "unfair dealing." Even in the large consol market, false prices are often successfully quoted; these, at one time, received the name of a certain Jobber, noted for the frequency of their occurrence from his reports to the marker.

It was alleged that a banking house dealt direct with this Jobber, and did not divide commission with a regular Broker. This gave rise to much scandal—not because the business was often done at one-eighth per cent. disadvantage, but on the grounds that the Brokers did not participate in the profits.

The case of Lodge, already referred to, as being before the City Court, the Court of Bankruptcy, and as one of "*public default,*" in which *all* redress had been exhausted by the Stock Exchange, presents also another strong feature. His name had been removed from the walls, and his sureties believed themselves absolved, when their letter of guarantee was produced, holding them liable for three years. They presented a petition to the Committee, denying the lengthened assurety, and alleging that there had been *fraud and forgery* of the letter. A commiseration vote of a meeting of the Stock Exchange creditors releasing them, saved the consistency of the Committee, and got rid of the charge.

The Committee have frequently ordered a holiday; and, in critical times, have required options to be declared on the day previous. No such matter could have occurred at Tattersall's, where gambling engagements, under the circumstances, would, by the laws of honor, have been void.

The Committee assume an important authority in the acknowledgment of new Companies; and in granting settlements of the early gambling transactions. The interests which direct them are shewn by the private Journal already quoted: "Recently, "many Companies have issued prospectuses for gold mining in "California. The shares of the first of these were in a few days "run up to 300 per cent. premium. It is believed that the Stock "Exchange, with the view to a 'rigg,' have bought more shares "than were issuable, or could be delivered—the number of Com- "panies has interfered with the design. It is hopeless to expect "the public to buy shares at a very high price in any one Com- "pany, and the chances are small of the Jobbers getting out."

"It is now said that the registration of these Companies is not "complete or regular, that the directors had no power to call the "full amount of the shares, but only the half per cent. prescribed "by the Act, that they are contrary to law in being issued as "scrip, &c., &c. It is supposed advantage may be taken of these "circumstances to *cancel all dealings*. This is singularly like "'*repudiation*,' a practice said never to be adopted by the Stock "Exchange. It is executed in this way:—on the issue of the "shares, the Committee adjourn the settlement *sine die*, and all "bargains necessarily fall to the ground. A gross case of this "kind occurred a few years ago, when several members of the "Committee were saved from ruin by the wholesale repudiation."

A few days later there is entered; "a '*row*' has taken place "to-day about West Mariposas, to exclude them from the Stock "Exchange, strong party-work is going on. The difficulty will "be to admit any of the Companies and to exclude others." Three days later; "The Committee have announced a settlement "in the West Mariposa Shares on the 25th inst, no other settle- "ment has yet been fixed; great exertions were made to fix the "Mariposa settlement, which will be against the public, on whom "the shares have been planted at a high premium; some of the "Committee are largely interested."

Again on the 26th; "The West Mariposa settlement was "effected yesterday so far as the payment of differences; but the "certificates not being ready, bonâ fide deliveries of Stock could "not be made in this hastened and premature settlement. The "open questions with regard to the others are yet undecided."

A further illustration of the motives and interests of the Association when ordering settlements, may be found in a private report of an abortive Company, read to a meeting of the shareholders convened on the 30th November, 1854. In the New South Wales Steam Coal and Navigation Company, £19,200 in money and in free shares had been charged to the Company for land in the colony, of which the *direct* purchase had been made for £2,500, and which had since been valued at £1 per acre, or £1,920; £6,000 had been paid to a Director for a vessel on sale for some months at £3,000, on which sum at least 10 per cent. discount would have been accepted. The enhanced price was explained by a statement that the vessel had changed hands several times, and the Voucher was explained to the Directors by the statement that it was by no means unusual for *Ship Brokers to make out a bill of sale with a higher price than that of the only contract to which they had been parties.* Further, that only £11,820 of the proposed £150,000 was received by the Company's bankers. The Directors then proceeded to "rigg" the market, by the purchase of 1,195 shares at a premium charged as a loss to the Company of nearly £600. They issued letters of allotment in fictitious names to represent 41,600 as having been paid upon, balancing the checks by other fictitious entries. A commission of £500 to the Brokers as well as the rigging profits, being £1,100 gain to the Association, a settlement was ordered and the shares of the Company were quoted in the daily Stock Exchange list. A similar exposure in the case of the Lake Bathurst Gold Company was made in the Court of Chancery.

Something of the process of "rigging" might be learned by reference to a trial when the High Sheriff of a metropolitan county and the ex-High Sheriff of another, received the severe admonition of H.M.'s Solicitor-General on the evidence he gave of his own dealings on the Stock Exchange.

Another hastened settlement is remembered in the Turkish Loan of 1852. No sooner was it known that no firman existed, than some influential members petitioned the Committee for a settlement, which was effected by the exchange of the deposit receipts. The Stock Exchange had boasted of the large proportion allotted to them. Some foreign buyers repudiated their purchases at 10 and 12 per cent. premium, on the grounds that no authorised Bond was given in exchange. Their agents outside had to bear the loss.

In the statement of the affairs of the Western Bank of London, it was shown that £1,000 had been paid to the chairman of the Stock Exchange as Broker; yet the directors with difficulty, and partly by bills, raised the first capital of £50,000. The fee received by this Broker and by others in public companies without any assistance in raising the capital, can only be looked upon as a bribe exacted by the Stock Exchange. The Ottoman Railway was admitted to the lists, these fees secured, and it was afterwards expunged. In the recent case of the Bank of Turkey a settlement of differences was hastened, and an order was issued that no shares should be bought in, the issue not being in convenient forms from the Company's office. The disgraceful proceedings in connection with this settlement were hushed up by the Press. In the Austrian Loan of 1859 buying-in was forbidden, to which the *Morning Post* honestly raised objections.

Sufficient has been said to show amply the nature of the self-protective laws, and their administration, to lead to a short notice of the constitution of the Association, and of its governing Committee. In the Association itself, there is no line of division between the classes. Mr. J. Capel, on the Exchequer Bill forgery inquiry, says:—"There are two distinct classes; some are Brokers, "*some are Jobbers, some mix the two characters.* I believe some "(Jobbers) take commission" (1661, 1662). Mr. Wm. Scott states he "is a Stockbroker and dealer in Exchequer Bills" (1805). Mr. Laurence tells the City Commission that "the Committee "is constituted not necessarily of Brokers, but of Brokers and "Jobbers" (4055 & 4056).

This Committee is secret in its sittings—irresponsible—refuses to hear aggrieved parties, not members, in person. No reasons for decisions are given to members, who being under absolute control can only carry clients' cases so far as the Committee choose to hear them. No appeal is permitted. Lastly, the Committee are judges in cases in which their own interests are concerned, individually and collectively, as members of the Association. The constitution of the Committee is of itself sufficient to account for its irregular proceedings. The Jobbers are dependent upon the Brokers, and cannot be supposed impartial judges in matters affecting their own supporters. Some are known to make a handsome income without the risk of trading, by "turns" given to them at the cost of Brokers' clients. It may be confidently asserted, that the more dishonest the practices of any Broker, the more certain he is to have secured a powerful party interest in the Committee.

This slight and inadequate exposure of the Stock Exchange, would not be complete without some allusion to the trade of the Jobber, a subject frequently brought forward by the writer in the *Daily News*—The "necessity" for the Stock Exchange, the "necessity" for Jobbers.

There is no space to enter fully into the abuses of this part of the system, beyond the hope of a notice sufficient to cause inquiry, before this denounced class may be stamped with legal recognition. It is alleged that the Jobber is useful to the public in being always a buyer or seller at a precarious profit difference. This is not so. The true Jobber's practice is, not to buy or sell until he has *read* his market and knows both buyer and seller. His interests lie in preventing buyers and sellers meeting, and to extort a large and unregulated profit. His object is to play on the limits of Brokers *confided* to him, or extorted from them it may be, where the Broker's credit and position is maintained by the Jobber. But in answer to the *Daily News* it may at once be said—that no Jobber is known in Paris, New York, or any other market; and the chief necessity in the London Stock Exchange will, it is believed, be found in the necessity to cover collusive fraud, on the part of the Brokers in a close market, with the certificate of respectability conferred by the Committee of the Stock Exchange.

Not long since, a leading jobbing firm made a price for French Railway obligations, so totally at variance with an almost fixed

Paris quotation that the seller applied to a friend, who, by direct correspondence with an Agent de Bourse, after payment of telegraphs and the cost of transmission, saved the seller above £70 on a £2,000 obligation. About the same time a Jobber in American Securities boasted that he had made a good profit that day of £120 between buying and selling a £3,000 or £4,000 Railway Bond; an extortion which it is apprehended has no parallel, and is scarcely equalled by the expenses of acquiring titles to freehold property, often referred to by quasi-reformers, members of these firms, who have gained admission to Parliament.

It is to be feared that collusion is frequent between brokers and jobbers, often occupying the same office: this has been sworn to in cases before chancery, it is believed there is often an arrangement between them. Bargains may be regularly booked, in order that the Broker may show a correctly kept "Broker's book" if called upon. And for the favors given to the jobber, ***he expects a cheque to be sent to him occasionally or periodically***, perhaps without reference to any one bargain, but a perfectly understood portion of the profit from the business he has brought to the jobber. A case is known where a deceased member was in the habit of receiving such profits unknown to his partners, till one of them came as executor to administer to his estate. It is, perhaps, not fully understood that jobbers are banded in sets, confining themselves perhaps to one stock; the *Daily News* itself has taken frequent notice of the jobbers in Joint Stock Bank shares, being unwilling to make "fair dealing prices."—Some time ago, on the occasion of two jobbers in Joint Stock Bank shares, out of only three, becoming defaulters, the Committee held the third responsible for all the losses. He had jobbed, in conjunction with the others during the "account." The Committee recommended jobbers acting in partnership to declare their mutual liability; an impracticable rule or recommendation which they could not enforce, and only a better cloak to collusion, where such jobbing was not declared; in this case the Committee interfered for the sake of character, or because the interests of an influential member was involved.

The Stock Exchange lose no occasion of advertising their Committee as a court of honor, &c., and from their numbers and power of dispensing favors, hold a powerful influence over the press, some portion of which always insert their letters, disowning outside parties brought before the courts of justice.

On the 28th October, 1858, a letter was addressed to the Lord Mayor, taking the better occasion of their formerly rebuked member being the head of the city, on the proceedings against William Lemon Oliver. "Many of our members have been much annoyed by parties calling themselves ***Stock Brokers, who "are not members of the Stock Exchange.***" This to the city, whom the Association defy and set at nought, was followed up by an *editorial* leader in the *Times*, on the 12th November, commencing :—" How is it that persons of real integrity, and sane mind, " &c. can be so ill advised as to employ Brokers *who are not members of the Stock Exchange*? The Commission charged, is " inconsiderable and trifling, when set against the security derived " from his position and responsibilities. The Committee exercise a " sharp surveillance over the members of the institution; they " have power to expel any member wno may be guilty of disgraceful or dishonourable conduct. * * * The Stock Exchange " divide their defaulters into three classes, &c. * * * The " wonder must ever be when transactions are so numerous, or of " such magnitude that so little *fraud is ever brought to light.* " There has been, however, before the public, a lamentable instance of the consequence of employing an *unauthorized and* " *irresponsible* person in place of a public Broker. All we can do " is to publish, from time to time, reports of notable frauds, and " to add that there are plenty of *regular* Brokers in the *city of* " *London*, who will transact business in a safe and satisfactory " manner, whilst thirty of the sharpest of their body, under the " name of the Committee, keep these gentlemen in order."

This article produced numerous letters in reply, and *The Times* found prudence in a guarded silence: but the *Daily News*, a Journal ot all times admitting Leaders and a City Article direct from the Stock Exchange, returns to the charge on the 26th November, more moderately, but with the phrases the " best " guarantee of respectability " and " certificate of respectability " conferred by the Stock Exchange.

In March, 1858, *The Times* prefaces a letter from the Stock Exchange in the City Article thus: " The following, from the " Committee of the Stock Exchange, furnishes an important " caution; persons are constantly spoken of as Brokers who are " not members of that establishment, and who are, therefore, not " in a position to give the public those guarantees of respectability of conduct which the stringent and excellent regulations " enforced *there are found to afford.*

At a recent date, a letter complained of the excessive charges of the Stock Exchange, and was followed next day by the City Article giving a Table of Commissions, varying from 10s. to £5 per cent., adding that these rates were really in accordance with their correspondent's wishes. *The Times* thus begging the question of the commissions being moderate, and advertising them as authorized, probably know that they were illegal, and were attracting attention, from the Paris Bourse having reduced their rate to 2s. per cent., and that the former rate of 2s. 6d. had been nearly the same as the legal charge authorised by the 10th Anne.

The Times does not publish at *any* time the "*notable frauds*" that come within its knowledge; and whilst holding the "*regular Brokers* "in the City, under the surveillance of *thirty of the sharpest,*" it must be presumed to know the irregular authority—both in fraudulent preference, and in the compromise of felony and misdemeanor—exercised by this *imperium in imperio,* the Committee, to obstruct the operation of both the civil and criminal law; otherwise that paper must shut itself out from the daily gossip of the City Coffee Houses.

Thirteen years ago, *The Times* commenced to publish the names of defaulters on the Stock Exchange, but soon desisted. On the 2nd May, 1859, it suggests the printing of the names of outside parties who might shew any disposition to sacrifice Brokers, but makes no mention of the wholesale repudiation of the Stock Exchange in that disgraceful panic partly precipitated by its celebrated "Russian Treaty" announcement.

Were *The Times* City writer to cease abusing a good "French "importation" of requiring deposits prior to the issue of Loans and of public Companies, because less profitable to the Stock Exchange and Stagg writers in the buying of allotment letters in the "rigging" process—were he to cease political writing in a purely commercial department of the paper, or cease to bait a Lord Advocate for not seeing it to be his duty "to hunt out crime," whilst he himself protects and advertises the Stock Exchange—he could furnish the ordinary editors with sufficient facts and scandals to supply leaders for a parliamentary recess, to fulfil their promise of exposing "notable frauds," *not* brought to light, in the Stock Exchange: he might save them braving the contempt of a high-minded nobleman and minister, attacked for placing a reserved price upon a fancy horse, repelled by the sale before the intended venomous but fangless pen was dry, and received by the public as the review of editorial spectacles in mirrored saloons, casting personal reflections and a present and a shadowed premier—or avoid their attacking merchants or Bill Brokers, for once, at least, at the risk of their litigious reputation to apologise when an equally heavy purse would meet them at law.

The Times is aware that credit is lower in the Stock Exchange, amongst themselves, than in any other mercantile body—that, in addition to the panic and seventy failures of May, 1859, there were thirty-seven failures *publicly* declared on another occasion; after which they wrote, on the 28th December, 1857: "Gambling, "compared with the Turf, the London Hells, and the German "Watering Places, sinks into insignificance. The result has been "the same as in the *more recognized resorts of sharpers and "blacklegs.*"

It will not deny that the Society exists by sufferance—that it even escapes from a disbelief in the possibility of the existence of so monstrous an institution—that the Committee are ever in fear of disaffected members exposing the system—that the responsibility divided amongst thirty of the "sharpest" of the "sharpers," permits at any time the absence of members who may know too much, and that those attending may never inconveniently hear enough to have their "consciences grievously offended"—that no one ever thinks it of the slightest use to urge any complaint against an influential member, though occasional scapegoats to character may be sacrificed in minor persons.

The Times may also be reminded that the evidence given by Mr. Lawrence before the City Inquiry Commission was taken into consideration at the time by the leaders of the Press, with a view to its exposure—which was not done.

Also that, in April, 1858, when the City Bill was before a Committee of the House of Commons, a letter was inserted in the leading columns, in the significant editorial type, a *feeler*, calling attention to the Bill proposing to abolish all control over Brokers; and it may be assured that, in the special case of Stock Brokers, there is a course open for its adoption, with an ample field for discussion and usefulness, and for enlisting popular sympathies; which may also help to develop the source of what it has called one of the scandals against this country, the discredit from railway management brought on foreign adventures, instancing Brazilian railways, "and that Holland is about to fall into the same "trap," the Jobbing system of the London Stock Exchange debarring persons holding them, from the extortionate cost of exchange. French Securities, to a certain extent, having only been successful from the ready access to the Paris Bourse, or through French bankers in Lendon. And when it may again have occasion to notice that the prime minister of Victoria had stated that the Stock Exchange was done, from Indian Loans being open, it may shew the Colonial Government the eventual quotations of their Securities, whenever the present financial operations are completed, and the market transactions have become limited.

If the Government of the British Colonial Empire are not successful in pressing upon the Home Government some interference and amendment of this world-wide scandal of England and the morality of its Legislature—it is worthy of the consideration of the Australian Colonies, appointing an Agency, or authorized Office of Registration in London, for the legitimate exchange of their Bonds, and their Home Incorporated and Guaranteed Companies; thereby largely tending to increase their own credit, by facilities and protection afforded to the public, who would eagerly take up subsequent loans on favorable terms.

The *Daily News* on the 12th March, 1860, brings forward a case of scandal occupying the attention of the Stock Exchange. "We have refrained alluding to it until it has become the topic "of common conversation. It is charged against a Broker of "*standing*, that he bought 100 shares in the market and himself "stood to 200, *giving the dealer's name for the 300 shares.* The "Committee should mark their sense of what is required for the "protection of the public, *who rely with justice upon the high* "*high character of the Stock Exchange*," Next day it says, "The Committee made an investigation, a resolution was *unani*-"*mously* passed to the effect that, the explanation given by the "firm, coupled with a letter from the principal, is *perfectly satis*-"*factory, exonerating* them from all blame. The client being "satisfied, no one else has any ground of complaint. In the "interest both of the public *and of the Stock Exchange*, which is "deservedly trusted by the public, the strict observance of the "relations between Broker and client cannot be too vigilantly "watched."

The parties alluded to, Messrs. D. & E., were sworn Brokers. Is any explanation consistent with the City obligations, or yet with the relations required by the equity and common law? Is it enough that one sharp client only should be satisfied? Is it satisfactory that they should be qualified to repeat this common practice under this added certificate, with the suppression of the evidence and their names, by a professedly to-be-trusted judicial private Committee?

Another not very dissimilar case can be substantiated, "yet not "brought to light." · · · · on the advice of his Brokers bought shares in the Rome and Frescati Railway; finding the price to be nominal and that they were unsaleable he instituted inquiries, and ascertained in the presence of a witness from the only Jobber in these shares, that no transaction had taken place in them for months. He demanded the name of the principal, and had given to him the Jobber who supplied this information. Under threats of resorting to the City Court, the Brokers, who are also of first reputed "standing," cancelled the bargain and refunded.

The insinuating mode of procedure of the Stock Exchange not only to gain, inch by inch, advantages over the Statute law, but also insidiously over the legislature and the Government, may be judged by the recent introduction of a new question. On the 14th February the *Times* inserted a letter on the penny stamp imposed by the budget on Stock Brokers contracts, and advocated the repeal of Sir J. Barnard's Act. Two days later a letter stated that the stamp was unnecesary, and the repeal of the Act of George II. is again urged as permitting unprincipled persons to commit frauds with impunity. The *Daily News* gave the clue by stating—"The Stock Exchange have delegated to a Sub-Com-"mittee to take steps for the abolition of the Barnard Act." On the same evening the Secretary to the Treasury in reply to Alderman Salomans, announced that the Act being obsolete, would be repealed as affecting the interests of the Stock Exchange, a respectable body of men.

The Under-Secretary might be reminded of the words of the ballad on the "Land Bank," about 1695;—

"What a negative law
To bind up the paw
Of legislative powers, Sir;
This is such a jest,
And so like the rest,
That sure it must be yours, Sir.

* * * *

This will do no good,
But you're lost in a wood,
And will run yourself a-ground, Sir.

A wood indeed of statutory laws, legal decisions, and of Stock Exchange practices. The Under Secretary himself at the bar surely knows that every statute, since the reign of William III, aimed at the correction of the abuses of Stock jobbing, and time bargains, and were rendered obsolete by the confederation of the Stock market about 60 years ago. He does not, however, propose the repeal of the 8th & 9th Vic. against wagering and gaming, ruling against the Stock Exchange in the case of Grisewood *v.* Blane, but over-ruled in so many recent decisions, that the legal profession now advise clients that the Stock Exchange can always establish their difference claims, except in the case of government Stocks, and can always repudiate claims under the "*regular mode of business.*" The mouth-piece of the Government, with all his personal experience of the Stock Exchange, in his connexion as Promoter and Director of the most speculative Companies, both home and foreign, formed within the last fifteen years, must be presumed fully cognisant of the advantages taken by the Stock Exchange, of the state of the law, and to have suspected that

"So cheats to play with those still aim,
That do not understand the game."

In so hurried an announcement. and as if a Government and a Chancellor of the Exchequer, with a new feature in a budget, were taken by surprise, is any guarantee to be given to the public of protection in the relations of Broker and client, or from a fraudulent misappropriation and preference of a self-constituted confederation, which might have been even for the time allowed to find out what was proper compliance with the law? When the members will still continue to issue stamped contract notes bearing their own scale of penal charges. Surely an additionol claim is due to the public, that the city should be heard on the question of licensing, when so established a principle of law, originally based upon national morality, has been overturned by a side wind pressure upon the Chancellor, fishing for a penny on his budget.

That the Barnard act in its application was effete, may be admitted, that it had been worse than useless might be contended, inasmuch as it had given occasion for the confederation of the Stock Exchange, by whom the disabilities have been turned into a collective advantage by systematic repudiation and fraudulent preference, not only in transactions in Government stocks, but in all dealings of shares in Joint Stocks.

The state of the law would appear to be; in the case of Grisewood *v.* Blane, a Stock Jobber was defeated on a contract in railway shares, under the 8th & 9th Vic. c. 109. It has been held by subsequent decisions, that a party who employs a Stock Broker to transact business for him *at a particular place is bound by the established usage of that place.* And that a Broker, under the usage of the Stock Exchange may recover differences, money paid to the use of his employer.

The removal of the only disability of the Stock Exchange, under the 7th & 8th Geo. II., will not lessen the disabilities of the public, against whom remain the 8th & 9th Vic. and the usage of the Stock Exchange.

A state of things worthy of more consideration than has been given to it, under the necessity of hasty legislation imposed by the Chancellor of Exchequer's budget, and raising the question, whether the usages of the Stock Exchange, are consistent with the spirit of the law, either legal or penal, as a subject for inquiry by Parliament or a special Commission, more particularly ere the enactments are repealed under the recommendation of the City Commission, and, whether it is not due to to the public to give opportunity to the city, to show the obstructions raised by the Stock Exchange to their authority. The more necessary from the *lâche* in the course of investigation of the Commission stated in the report, page 10. " We shall confine ourselves to those institutions " which form a part of the City of London, or are *necessarily* " *connected,* and therefore we shall say nothing of trading com- " panies which are not constituent parts of the Corporation." A line of restriction by which the Commission was deprived of the power of hearing explanations of evidence, adopted by them as the grounds of the report, and received from such a body formed within the city and the only class having a building appropriated to business, who raised objections to the city authority. Every market, under the special direction of the city, Newgate, Billingsgate, &c., was inquired into, and the Coal market with reference to city dues, but not with regard to its constitution and regulations under the city. This is to be regretted, as in case of the city having shown a beneficial jurisdiction in the registratiou of transactions, &c., a precedent might have been found for the constitution of a Stock market, or even as the Corn market, under the 47 Geo. III. c. 68, required to be a "*free, open, and public market.*"

A plan for a Stock market might be given, but it is not intended to prejudge this question which has been one of difficulty and special legislation in all neighbouring countries, and the question therefore of securities need not be touched, except so far as this part of the subject was brought before the Commission, Mr. Auckland says, Brokers give security for a most inefficient amount; the licence should be effective as a guarantee against mal-practices. (535) In the case of Rochas and Son, the loss and actual fraud was only 2s. 6d. upon 100 shares, or £12 10s.; and in the recent case, so fully exonerated by the Stock Exchange Committee, the loss on 300 Bank of Turkey shares, even on cancelling the transaction could not be supposed excessive. The disqualification from continuing a petty system of fraud it is conceived is more important in itself than individual redress, even in great public defaults, of which the Stock Exchange could show a full share.

It is unnecessary, in the position of the question, to say to what authority, as more efficient and responsible than the city, should be entrusted the licensing of Brokers, unless the Lords of the Treasury were to undertake the trust as in the reign of Anne, and to hold it in suspense pending the possible creation of a chamber of Commerce, a reform almost as hopeless as it was in the day of Samuel Lambe, who proposed to the Lord Protector in 1658 "a "Court of Merchants for settling controversies at small cost; *a "modell whereof, I have ready to produce when called thereunto.*"

One other matter requires some notice. It is the assertion often heard from the Stock Exchange directly and indirectly, that it is not only tolerated, but secretly supported by all the Governments of the Country from necessity, and to avoid embarrassment in placing a large amount of new Stock; were there any truth in the assertion, beyond the impudence of the originators, made to strengthen and raise the Association in the estimation of the Public, experience might be appealed to. During the early contraction of the national debt, and at the period of the loyalty loan of 1797, the Stock Exchange was unknown. In the first fifteen years of its existence, the national credit was pledged at a lower price than at any period of its history.

The first English loan of 1855 during the Crimean War, attained 6 per cent. premium within three months. In the two loans of 1856, the Chancellor of the Exchequer obtained by adhering to his limit, $\frac{7}{8}$ per cent. on the first, and more than 1 per cent. on the second above the price of the only tenders, and this advance the Contractor was prepared to concede on the spot to the firmness of the Minister. These loans always maintained a premium to justify the assertion that by an open appeal to the Country more favorable terms might have been obtained. It is known, that in 1855 the Minister's attention was drawn to the machinery of the Savings'

Banks being adapted to the purpose of extending the sphere of subscriptions in being authorised to receive deposits.

France has shown an example of what a nation can effect towards its Governmental deficiencies, in both the Crimean and Italian wars.

Fundings during peace might be referred to, in 1841 the Government of Sir R. Peel declined the biddings of the large contractors and opened subscriptions at the Bank of England. The great success of the recent Indian loan is not very flattering to the Minister, an old Chancellor of the Exchequer in the low price to which the Stock Exchange had forced the quotation before the tenders were opened.

Moreover, contractors for all recent loans have required from subscribers full payment of the Government deposit, thereby doing away with the only value of the present mode, in holding a contractor responsible. The terms of late loans involving only the forfeiture of the deposit.

The want of a Public Stock market assumes the greatest appearance of absurdity; when it is shown that the Chancellor of Exchequer on occasions of Public financing, writes to the Governors of the Bank of England to request them to announce in "*the usual manner*"; the law which required an intimation of the Government to redeem the 3 per cent. consols, to be posted for six months on the walls of the Royal Exchange must have contemplated an open market, and scarcely that Government measures should be conveyed through a close Association, or on the second day to the public through the medium of the Press. That an open market incorporated by Parliament, and subject to some superior authority is alone consistent with the spirit of the Country is a question which does not require to be argued. But to give substantiality to the view that an open Stock Exchange is compatible with the spirit of the present statute laws, it may be stated, that on the close of the war which replaced the Bourbon family on the throne of France; the Stock Exchange Committee disowned dealings in French Rentes, and a voluntary market arose in the Royal Exchange and elsewhere, which engrossed a larger amount of business than the Association. The Committee having seen their mistake invited these outside Brokers into the Association, setting aside the ordinary rules of admission. Again in Liverpool for ten years previous to 1844, a number of share Brokers were excluded from a small Association, founded on rules similar to the London Stock Exchange, a coalition took place, only after the outside market had become stronger both in numbers and in wealth than the old Association.

Should the Government refuse an inquiry into the usages of the Stock Exchange, the question is one well worthy the attention of the Social Science Association, and it may be hoped that if an

www.ingramcontent.com/pod-product-compliance
Lightning Source LLC
LaVergne TN
LVHW052020160826
845678LV00003B/1139

* 9 7 8 0 3 5 3 5 4 2 8 6 0 *